CONNECTED PLAYBOOK

ANNA GOODMAN
ILLUSTRATED BY ASHLEY SIMPKINS

Text © 2022 Anna Goodman
Illustrations © 2022 Ashley Simpkins

All rights reserved. Except for brief excerpts for review purposes, no part of this book may be reproduced or used in any form without written permission from the author.

The rights of Anna Goodman to be identified as the author and Ashley Simpkins to be identified as the illustrator have been asserted by them in accordance with the Copyright, Design and Patents Act 1988.

All Scripture quotations, unless otherwise indicated, are taken from the New International Version Copyright 1973, 1978, 1984, 2011 by Biblica, Inc..

Cover Design by Daniel Goodman, Dan Gould and Ashley Simpkins

ISBN 979-8-47192-069-9

First Published in 2022 by Amazon
Printed in the United Kingdom

WELCOME!

This is sequel to our previous book, *"Connected: God's quiet voice in a world that shouts"*. When I originally wrote the title, I called this a 'workbook' because, quite simply, it is a book to write in and engage with. But something about that didn't feel right. A workbook implies work. What's so important and different about the Christian faith is that it's a relationship built entirely on grace and not our works[1]. So I decided against calling this a workbook.

John Wimber said, *"Everyone gets to play".* One of the things he tried to teach those around him was that we all get to do the things that Jesus did because all Christians have the Holy Spirit in them. We can all hear God's voice and be obedient to His words. Everyone gets to be involved in God's plans, not just *'special people'!*

So this is a 'playbook'. It's a book that's supposed to be enjoyable and it's a book that will help you, a child of God, grow in how you listen and learn to respond to your Father's voice as you *give it a go*.

Let the fun begin.

Love,

Anna

---

[1] *"For it is by grace you have been saved, through faith - and this is not from yourselves, it is a gift from God - not by works, so that no one can boast."* (Ephesians 2:8-9)

BE, HAVE, DO

"God decided in advance to adopt us into his own family by bringing us to himself through Jesus Christ. This is what he wanted to do, and it gave him great pleasure."
Ephesians 1:5 (NLT)

In modern life, many of us believe that we have to do something in order to have something so that we can be someone. But that's not God's way. In His Kingdom it's the other way around. As soon as you become a Christian, you are adopted into God's family. You are His child, that is your new identity without earning it. You do not need to strive for His affection. You do not need to prove anything to Him.

REFLECT
Look at your life right now. Ask the Holy Spirit to show you if you are striving to earn God's acceptance and approval.

ACT
Ask the Father to show you the truth; that He already really loves you and there's nothing you need to do to earn His love.

FILL THE ARROW TO INDICATE YOUR LEVEL OF STRIVING

Date ____ / ____ / ____

CONNECTED?

"I am the vine; you are the branches. If you remain in me and I in you, you will bear much fruit; apart from me you can do nothing."
John 15:5

Every millisecond of every day, your brain is in continual communication with your whole body in order to keep it alive and functioning as it should. Sometimes, however, these signals get disrupted and this can cause problems. Similarly, we were created to live in constant communion with our Heavenly Father. However, sometimes the way we choose to live our lives makes us feel detached and disconnected from God and this can have a negative impact on our spiritual health.

REFLECT
On a scale of 0-10 how connected do you feel to God right now?

ACT
What one simple habit can you start today that will help you feel more connected to God? e.g. You could intentionally remember to talk to Him each time you boil the kettle.

MARK ON THIS SCALE HOW CONNECTED YOU FEEL TO GOD.

WEEK 0 | 1 | 2 | 3 | 4 | 5 | 6 | 7 | 8 | 9 | 10 |

WEEK 4 | 1 | 2 | 3 | 4 | 5 | 6 | 7 | 8 | 9 | 10 |

Date _____ / _____ / _____

CHILDREN OF GOD

"See what great love the Father has lavished on us, that we should be called children of God! And that is what we are!"
1 John 3:1

God is our loving Father and we are His precious children. But sometimes it's hard to understand what a perfect Father would be like because of our own experiences.

REFLECT
Spend some time reflecting on your own story. How has this influenced the way you expect God the Father to be with you?
Pray about these things.

ACT
Write down two lists:
1) What your father is/was like
2) What God the Father is like.

Compare the two.

MY FATHER	GOD THE PERFECT FATHER
	GOD IS LOVE (1 JOHN 4:8) GRACIOUS AND COMPASSIONATE, SLOW TO ANGER, ABOUNDING IN LOVE AND FAITHFULNESS (EXODUS 34:6).

Date _____ / _____ / _____

NAMES OF GOD

"God said to Moses, "I AM WHO I AM. This is what you are to say to the Israelites: 'I AM has sent me to you.'"
Exodus 3:14

Scripture uses many names to describe different aspects of God's nature and character.

REFLECT
Spend some time reflecting on the names of God.

ACT
Ask the Holy Spirit which name He wants to speak to you about right now.

Highlight it and ask Him why it's important.

EL SHADDAI (LORD GOD ALMIGHTY) – GENESIS 17:1
EL ELYON (THE MOST HIGH GOD) – GENESIS 14:18-20
ADONAI (LORD, MASTER) – GENESIS 15:2
YAHWEH (LORD, JEHOVAH) – GENESIS 2:4
JEHOVAH NISSI (THE LORD MY BANNER) – EXODUS 17:15-16
JEHOVAH-RAAH (THE LORD MY SHEPHERD) – PSALM 23:1
JEHOVAH RAPHA (THE LORD THAT HEALS) – 2 KINGS 20:5
JEHOVAH SHAMMAH (THE LORD IS THERE) – EZEKIEL 48:35
JEHOVAH TSIDKENU (THE LORD OUR RIGHTEOUSNESS) – JEREMIAH 23:6
JEHOVAH MEKODDISHKEM (THE LORD WHO SANCTIFIES YOU) – EXODUS 31:13
EL OLAM (THE EVERLASTING GOD) – GENESIS 21:33
ELOHIM (GOD) – GENESIS 1:1
QANNA (JEALOUS) – EXODUS 20:5
JEHOVAH JIREH (THE LORD WILL PROVIDE) – GENESIS 22:14
JEHOVAH SHALOM (THE LORD IS PEACE) – JUDGES 6:24
JEHOVAH SABAOTH (THE LORD OF HOSTS) – 1 SAMUEL 1:3
EL ROI (THE GOD WHO SEES ME) – GENESIS 16:13

Date _____ / _____ / _____

QUIET WATERS

"He leads me beside quiet waters, he refreshes my soul."
Psalm 23:2-3

Did you know that when your body is stressed, the extra adrenaline can decrease the blood circulation to your ears, reducing your ability to hear?

Anxiety or stress can also make it harder to hear God's voice. Having a peaceful heart helps us to hear God more clearly.

REFLECT
Imagine looking at the surface of a river that reflects how you are feeling. Are the waves choppy or is the water calm and quiet?

ACT
Psalm 131:2 says, "I have calmed and quieted myself". If your 'waters' feel stormy, take some time and ask the Holy Spirit why you are feeling this way. Then ask Him to fill you with His peace.

Date _____ / _____ / _____

ALONE

"He went up on a mountainside by himself to pray"
Matthew 14:22

Matthew 14 is a dramatic chapter in the Bible. It tells us about a beheading, how Jesus miraculously fed five thousand men, walked on water, calmed a storm and finally, healed a great number of people. However, interspersed within the drama are crucial clues to Jesus' way of life and His priorities: "he withdrew from there in a boat to a desolate place by himself" and "he went up on the mountain by himself to pray."

Jesus withdrew from others and spent time alone talking with the Father.

REFLECT
Jesus often withdrew from others and spent time alone talking with the Father.

How much time do you spend with God by yourself?

ACT
Ask God to help you make one change to your lifestyle today that will help you have more time with Him.

HELP ME

START
✓ _____
✓ _____
✓ _____

STOP
✗ _____
✗ _____
✗ _____

Date _____ / _____ / _____

THE BUZZING FLY

"I am saying this for your own good, not to restrict you, but that you may live in a right way in undivided devotion to the Lord."
1 Corinthians 7:35

A distraction is anything that prevents you from concentrating on something, such as a buzzing fly! Sometimes these things will be out of your control, but other times we can take practical steps to remove or minimise them.

REFLECT
What things do you think are causing you to lose your attention when listening to God?

ACT
Choose one distraction. Identify one step that you can take that will help you minimise that distraction.
E.g. Put your phone in another room whilst praying.

Date _____ / _____ / _____

A RAIN DROP

"And after the fire came a gentle whisper. When Elijah heard it, he pulled his cloak over his face and went out and stood at the mouth of the cave. Then a voice said to him, "What are you doing here, Elijah?""
1 Kings 19:12-13

Would you notice a single raindrop falling on your skin? Sometimes God's voice can be as subtle as that; as quiet as a whisper.

REFLECT
Ask God to help you notice the small things so you can hear His soft whisper.

ACT
What steps can you take to create a quiet heart and mind?

Date ____ / _____ / _____

DISCONNECT

"Now devote your heart and soul to seeking the Lord your God."
1 Chronicles 22:19

How much time are you spending on your phone? Most phones have a setting that will show you this information and even what apps were being used!

REFLECT
Are you using your time wisely?

ACT
Record your phone usage everyday this week. Perhaps you could try having a simple rule like 'no phones before 9am or after 8pm'?

MON	____ h	____ m
TUES	____ h	____ m
WED	____ h	____ m
THURS	____ h	____ m
FRI	____ h	____ m
SAT	____ h	____ m
SUN	____ h	____ m

Date _____ / _____ / _____

SELF AWARE

"Then he returned to his disciples and found them sleeping."
Matthew 26:40

Imagine having a conversation with a friend who kept falling asleep! Do you think this would make you upset? Would you feel like they didn't value you or that they were being rude?

REFLECT
When do you normally engage with God in an intentional way? Is it when you're tired or sleepy? Or when you're alert and attentive?

God deserves your best.

ACT
Mark out your 24 hr energy levels. Identify your highest and lowest energy points. Then mark when you normally spend time with God. Can you change your routine so that God gets you at your best?

high energy

low energy

1 2 3 4 5 6 7 8 9 10 11 12 1 2 3 4 5 6 7 8 9 10 11 12

Date _____ / _____ / _____

A FARMER'S FIELD

"A farmer went out to sow his seed..."
Matthew 13:3

Imagine a field full of produce. The crops represent things in your life that God is blessing. The rocks represent things that are preventing your roots (or relationship with God) from growing deeper. The weeds are things around you that are taking your attention away from God. Finally, the sun represents people or habits that are feeding your spiritual growth. Sometimes it's worth intentionally taking time to assess what the field of our life looks like.

REFLECT
Can you identify your sun, crops, rocks and weeds?

ACT
Fill in the diagram to illustrate what's going on in your life.

Pray about each area.

FEEDING:

CROPS

WEEDS:

ROCKS:

Date ____ / ____ / ____

THE HOLY KING

"At the name of Jesus every knee should bow, in heaven and on earth and under the earth, and every tongue acknowledge that Jesus Christ is Lord, to the glory of God the Father."
Philippians 2:10-11

Sometimes we can focus too much on the fact that Jesus is our friend and forget that He is also our King. Not only is He a King, He is the King of kings and Lord of lords (Revelation 19:16). God is also utterly and entirely holy. Isaiah 6:3 says, "Holy, holy, holy is the LORD Almighty; the whole earth is full of his glory."

REFLECT
Spend some time in quietness focusing on the fact that Jesus is King over all creation. Imagine approaching Him in His throne room.

ACT
Read Revelation 4.

How do you feel? Try to keep hold of that sense of awe and reverence as you talk to Him today (and everyday).

Date _____ / _____ / _____

VOICE RECOGNITION

"His sheep follow him because they know his voice. But they will never follow a stranger; in fact, they will run away from him because they do not recognize a stranger's voice."
John 10:4-5

There will always be many 'voices' in your head; your parents, teachers, friends, critics, workmates - the list is endless. What is important is learning how to work out who they belong to. Some of the voices will need to be rejected and ignored. Some of them will be full of lies. But in amongst those voices will be God's and it will take careful time and attention to work out which one belongs to Him.

REFLECT
Whose voice do you think is loudest in your head? Is it God's, your own or other's?

Knowing your Bible will help you discern these voices more easily.

ACT
Highlight the statements that you think are from God the Father.

"YOU ARE SO PRECIOUS"
"I'M ASHAMED OF YOU"
"YOU ARE A FAILURE"
"I LOVE WATCHING YOU GROW!"
"YOU ARE A KIND PERSON"
"I'M SO PROUD OF YOU"
"YOU ARE ALWAYS MAKING STUPID MISTAKES"
"IF OTHER PEOPLE REALLY KNEW WHAT YOU WERE LIKE THEY WOULDN'T LOVE YOU"
"YOU WILL NEVER CHANGE"
"I WILL NEVER ABANDON YOU"
"YOU ARE HOPELESS"
"YOU HAVE LET ME DOWN"
"YOU BRING ME SO MUCH JOY!"
"YOU ARE A NASTY PERSON"
"I AM DISAPPOINTED IN YOU"
"YOU ARE UNLIKE ANYONE ELSE IN THE WORLD."
"YOU WILL NEVER BE GOOD ENOUGH"

Date ____ / _____ / _____

CONSTANT CHAT

"Rejoice always, pray continually, give thanks in all circumstances; for this is God's will for you in Christ Jesus."
1 Thessalonians 5:16-18

Bankers don't spot forgeries by spending endless hours studying fake money. They're able to spot forgeries easily because they spend so much time around genuine bank notes. They know what authentic money looks like because they're with it the whole time. So too, with God. The more time you spend with God, the quicker you will be at recognising when He is speaking to you and when He's not, when it's your own thoughts and when it's His.

REFLECT
How often do you pray throughout the day? Are you in continual conversation with God?

ACT
The Holy Spirit is always with you. Dedicate one day to Him where you aim to talk to Him as much as possible. What was your experience like? Do you want to continue living your life that way?

RECORD your EXPERIENCE HERE ↻

Date _____ / _____ / _____

A LAMP

"The eye is the lamp of the body. If your eyes are healthy, your whole body will be full of light."
Matthew 6:22

Everything you listen to and watch has an impact on you. Think about a lamp. It might have the brightest light inside it, but if the glass is all sooty and black, hardly any of the light will be able to pass through. Sin can be a bit like the soot on the glass of our lives that prevents the bright light of Jesus shining through you onto the world around you.

REFLECT
Meditate on Ephesians 5:8-11.
"Live as children of light (for the fruit of the light consists in all goodness, righteousness and truth) and find out what pleases the Lord."

ACT
Ask the Holy Spirit to highlight anything that you are currently watching or listening to that is adding soot to your glass. Are you willing to give these things up?

Date _____ / _____ / _____

BRAIN SURGERY

"Be transformed by the renewing of your mind."
Romans 12:2

There's an old saying in neuroscience that says, "neurons that fire together, wire together." What this means is that the more you have a thought, the stronger the nerve connections linked to that thought become. The opposite is also true. When you stop thinking a certain way, that nerve pathway become weaker. Choosing what we do and do not think about therefore changes the wiring in our brain.

REFLECT
The Bible tells us how to think like Jesus. When we read it often, the Holy Spirit uses it to change the way we think.

ACT
What are you thinking about often? What thoughts do you want to have less of?

WRITE HERE
THOUGHTS you
WANT TO HAVE
MORE OF

WRITE HERE
THOUGHTS you
WANT TO HAVE
LESS OF

Date _____ / _____ / _____

THE SWORD

"Jesus answered, "It is written: 'Man shall not live on bread alone, but on every word that comes from the mouth of God.'"
Matthew 4:4

Matthew 4 tells the story of when Jesus was tempted in the desert. Each time Jesus was tempted by satan, He replied, *"It is written…"* and then quoted from scripture. His weapon to fight satan was God's written Word.

REFLECT
This passage shows us that the way to fight spiritual attack is by knowing the truth contained in Scripture. Jesus was able to do this because He had memorised it.

ACT
Spend some time today choosing a verse that has meaning to you.

Throughout your week, try to commit it to memory and remind yourself of it often.

Date ____ / _____ / _____

PROMISES

"Does he speak and then not act? Does he promise and not fulfill?"
Numbers 23:19

I don't know about you, but I have broken a lot of promises in my life. Sometimes it was unintentional but other times it was because I was flippant with my words and never really intended to fulfil the promises I made. Unlike us, however, God doesn't speak in haste and always stands by His words.

"I the LORD have spoken it, and will do it." Ezekiel 22:14.

REFLECT
Do you have any promises that you feel as though God has spoken to you but haven't yet been fulfilled?

ACT
Write down these promises.

Now talk to Him about it/them. Thank Him that He is a faithful God and ask Him to help you trust Him in the waiting.

Date _____ / _____ / _____

VERSE OF THE YEAR

"The hand of the LORD was on me there, and he said to me, "Get up and go out to the plain, and there I will speak to you.""
Ezekiel 3:22

God knows your past, your present and your future. Sometimes, if we ask Him, we might find that He wants to give us a specific Bible verse that is important for us to focus on in the year and season ahead. Since God knows what you're going to have to face and where things will be difficult, being guided to specific wisdom and truth found in His Word can be very helpful to hold on to during these times.

REFLECT
Ask the Holy Spirit to show you whether there is a verse that He wants you to specifically meditate on at the moment.

ACT
Write down the passage. Try to access different Bible translations of the same verse.

Ask God why He's given it to you and why it's important.

MY VERSE of 20__ IS

_____

_____

_____

_____   _____

_____   _____

write it in
a different version ↙   and another ↑

Date _____ / _____ / _____

INNERMOST DETAIL

"You have searched me, Lord, and you know me."
Psalm 139:1

God knows everything about you. Everything. He knows how many grams of chocolate you've eaten in your entire lifetime, whether your stomach grumbled when you read that last sentence or if, in fact, you're diabetic.

He is the only one who really knows the true you.

REFLECT
Read through Psalm 139 slowly three times.

ACT
Ask the Holy Spirit to highlight one line that He wants you to focus on right now.

Ask Him why. Try to memorise that verse.

You have searched me, Lord, and you know me.
You know when I sit and when I rise;
you perceive my thoughts from afar.
You discern my going out and my lying down;
you are familiar with all my ways.
Before a word is on my tongue
you, Lord, know it completely.
You hem me in behind and before,
and you lay your hand upon me.
Such knowledge is too wonderful for me,
too lofty for me to attain.
Where can I go from your Spirit?
Where can I flee from your presence?
If I go up to the heavens, you are there;
if I make my bed in the depths, you are there.
If I rise on the wings of the dawn,
if I settle on the far side of the sea,
even there your hand will guide me,
your right hand will hold me fast.
If I say, "Surely the darkness will hide me
and the light become night around me,"
even the darkness will not be dark to you;
the night will shine like the day,
for darkness is as light to you.
For you created my inmost being;
you knit me together in my mother's womb.
I praise you because I am fearfully and wonderfully made;
your works are wonderful,
I know that full well.
My frame was not hidden from you
when I was made in the secret place,
when I was woven together in the depths of the earth.
Your eyes saw my unformed body;
all the days ordained for me were written in your book
before one of them came to be.
How precious to me are your thoughts, God!
How vast is the sum of them!

Date ____ / ____ / ____

THE CREATOR

"So whether you eat or drink or whatever you do, do it all for the glory of God."
1 Corinthians 10:31

God created everything. One of the lies we can sometimes believe is that certain areas of our lives are less spiritual than others. There is no sacred vs. secular divide to God. Work, art, holidays, family, Bible study, serving - they all matter to Him. Every part of your life needs God. Everything is sacred. Everything can be done for His glory.

REFLECT
There's no area of our lives that God doesn't have an opinion about. When we intentionally include Him in everything, we can start to see things the way He does.

ACT
Is there any aspect of your life that you don't think God is interested in? Invite Him to join you in that area. Ask Him for His perspective.

↑ ASPECT OF YOUR LIFE

I INVITE GOD INTO IT

Date ____ / _____ / _____

MOTHER TONGUE

"Once again, the kingdom of heaven is like a net that was let down into the lake and caught all kinds of fish."
Matthew 13:47

In Scripture, we see how Jesus used parables about fishing when connecting to fishermen. He knew what 'language' to speak in order to get His message across. The same goes for you. If you know lots about the outdoors, He may well use analogies involving tents and camping gear in order to share His heart with you. God knows what you will and will not understand.

REFLECT
What do you love? If God was to use a language based on things that you are interested in, what language would that be?

ACT
Spend some time asking God whether He wants to speak to you using a particular metaphor that you will understand.

I LOVE...

♥ _____

♥ _____

♥ _____

♥ _____

♥ _____

Date ____ / _____ / _____

MEMORIES

"I will remember the deeds of the LORD"
Psalm 77:11

One of the earliest memories I can recall is of the smell of the dust on the streets of Nepal. I would have been about 4 years old at the time. Incredibly, however, we actually first start creating memories whilst we're still in the womb. Even though you will forget much of what you have stored in your brain, God doesn't. He knows each and every one of the memories we have ever had or indeed will ever have.

REFLECT
Spend some time asking God to bring into your mind a specific memory that He wants to talk to you about.

ACT
Once you think you have one, ask God what He wants to say about it. What is His perspective?

MEMORY

GOD SAID...

Date _____ / _____ / _____

KNOWLEDGE

"The heart of the discerning acquires knowledge, for the ears of the wise seek it out."
Proverbs 18:15

God knows every bit of information that you know and have ever learnt. He knows all the places you've visited, all the skills you've developed, all the mistakes you've made and all the cereal boxes you've read - everything! He can use any of that information to speak to you.

REFLECT
Does it surprise you that God can use the facts and lessons that you have learnt in order to communicate to you?

ACT
Why don't you spend some time asking God to speak to you through something that you have discovered recently.

Date _____ / _____ / _____

DREAMS

"In the last days, God says, I will pour out my Spirit on all people. Your sons and daughters will prophesy, your young men will see visions, your old men will dream dreams"
Acts 2:17

Have you ever had a dream that just stands out somehow? Sometimes the Holy Spirit speaks to us through our dreams. It's good to get into the habit of recording them just in case God decides that He wants to speak to you when you are asleep!

REFLECT
Are you someone who remembers their dreams easily? Do you think that God has ever tried to say anything through one/some of them?

ACT
This week, ask the Holy Spirit to speak to you as you sleep. Write down your dreams and ask God about them!

DREAM

I ASKED...

GOD SAID...

Date ____ / ____ / ____

AN EMOTIONAL GOD

"When Jesus landed and saw a large crowd, he had compassion on them and healed their sick."
Matthew 14:14

According to the Oxford English Dictionary, compassion is 'the feeling or emotion, when a person is moved by the suffering or distress of another, and by the desire to relieve it.'

We read in Scripture how Jesus was often moved with compassion and how He acted in these moments.

REFLECT
Have you ever noticed times when you feel things that don't seem like they have come from you? Perhaps you've had an insight into what God's emotions are.

ACT
This week as you go about your normal life, try to be sensitive to God guiding you by His compassion. Does He want you to do anything in response? Write your experience here.

HEART of compassion

Date _____ / _____ / _____

WALKING, TALKING GOD

"And surely I am with you always, to the very end of the age."
Matthew 28:20

Everywhere we go, God walks with us. He is our constant companion. This means that, just in the same way as a friend might comment on something as you pass by, God might want to use the world around you, in order to say something to you.

REFLECT
Do you expect God to speak to you at any time in the day, wherever you go? Are you always listening?

ACT
Today, why don't you intentionally notice what is happening around you? Does the Holy Spirit seem to be highlighting anything? If so, ask Him what He wants to say.

I NOTICED...

GOD SAID...

Date _____ / _____ / _____

GOD'S INVISIBLE QUALITIES

"For since the creation of the world God's invisible qualities—his eternal power and divine nature—have been clearly seen, being understood from what has been made, so that people are without excuse."
Romans 1:20

God is The Creator. His creation gives us glimpses about who He is. Galaxies tell us about His greatness. Rainbows remind us of His faithfulness. Wind works to show us His invisible power. Light leads us to grasp His brilliance.

REFLECT
Do you easily see God's signature and character in the natural world around you?

ACT
Set aside some time today to be outdoors. Ask God to speak to you about His character.

Date ____ / _____ / _____

CONNECTIONS

"As Jesus was walking beside the Sea of Galilee, he saw two brothers, Simon called Peter and his brother Andrew. They were casting a net into the lake, for they were fishermen. "Come, follow me," Jesus said."
Matthew 4:18-19

God cares about the relationships and friendships that we have. After all, Jesus handpicked his own disciples! Sometimes God is purposefully bringing people into our lives for a specific reason. He is deliberately setting us up...

REFLECT
Think about all the different relationships you have in your life at the moment, from mere acquaintances to deep friendships.

ACT
Spend some time asking God which relationships are important to focus on right now. Prioritise and invest in those connections. Make Jesus central to them. Glorify Him through them.

Date ____ / ____ / ____

EPHPHATHA

"He looked up to heaven and with a deep sigh said to him, "Ephphatha!" (which means "Be opened!"). At this, the man's ears were opened, his tongue was loosened and he began to speak plainly."
Mark 7:34-35

"Sorry"
"Help!"
"GO."
"Please?" A single word can be very powerful.

"Open." Jesus caused a deaf and mute man to be able to hear and speak with one of His words. Isn't that incredible?

REFLECT
Are you someone who uses a lot of words?

Sometimes words lose their power if there are too many of them.

ACT
Ask God for one, single word that He wants to say to you right now. Then ask Him for His perspective on that word. Why is it important to Him? Why is it important for you?

ONE WORD...

Date _____ / _____ / _____

CHANGING SHOES

"I will instruct you and teach you in the way you should go; I will counsel you with my loving eye on you."
Psalm 32:8

If you go into a shoe shop you'll notice that there's a really wide variety available. Different shoes are appropriate for different activities and locations. We wear walking boots if we're climbing up mountains, but we wear flip-flops to the beach.

Looking at someone's shoes can indicate where they've been or where they are about to go.

REFLECT
What kind of season are you in right now? Are things easy or hard? Do you feel like you are struggling to stand, or do you feel firmly grounded?

ACT
Ask God what kind of 'shoes' are appropriate for you at the moment. What comes into your mind? Ask Him why that particular pair is relevant to you and draw them here.

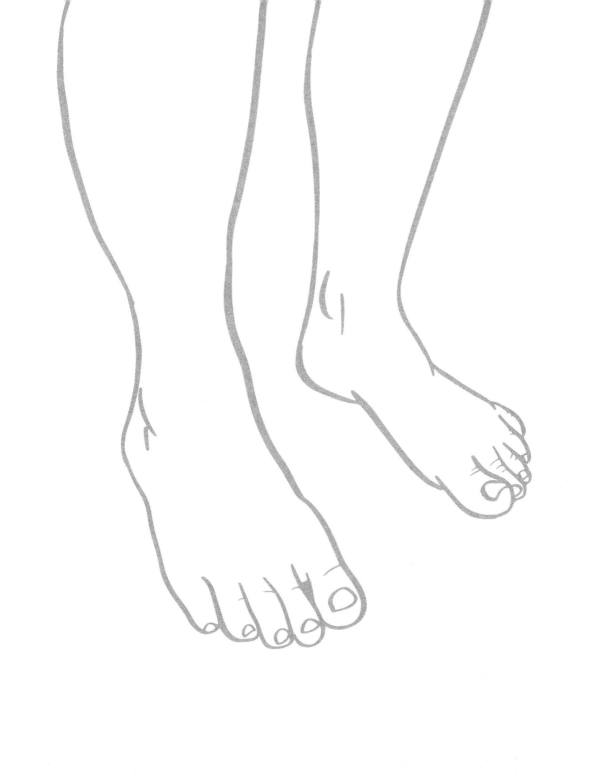

Date _____ / _____ / _____

GOD WINKS

"I will lead the blind by ways they have not known, along unfamiliar paths I will guide them; I will turn the darkness into light before them and make the rough places smooth. These are the things I will do; I will not forsake them."
Isaiah 42:16

Sometimes God gives us little confirmations in our lives to reassure us that we are on the right track and that He is with us. Different people may use different language for this - 'God winks', 'breadcrumbs' and 'God's fingerprints' are just a few examples I've heard!

REFLECT
Pause and look back over your life. Can you see little encouragements from God that have helped you know He is walking with you, guiding you?

ACT
It's easy to forget the times and ways God has helped direct us. Why don't you write them down so that you can remember them. Then spend some time thanking God.

Date _____ / _____ / _____

RECORD KEEPERS

"Write in a book all the words I have spoken to you."
Jeremiah 30:2

In the Bible we read how God was continuously faithful to His people. He told them to record their journey; what He had done for them and what He had asked them to do. Not only would this help them to remember, but it also meant they could pass it on to their children.

REFLECT
What stories has God given you in your journey with Him? Do you think that it would be worth sharing some of them with others in order to encourage them?

ACT
Start a book to help you keep track of your journey with God. Try to remember to keep looking back on what you've written. What have you learnt? How have things changed?

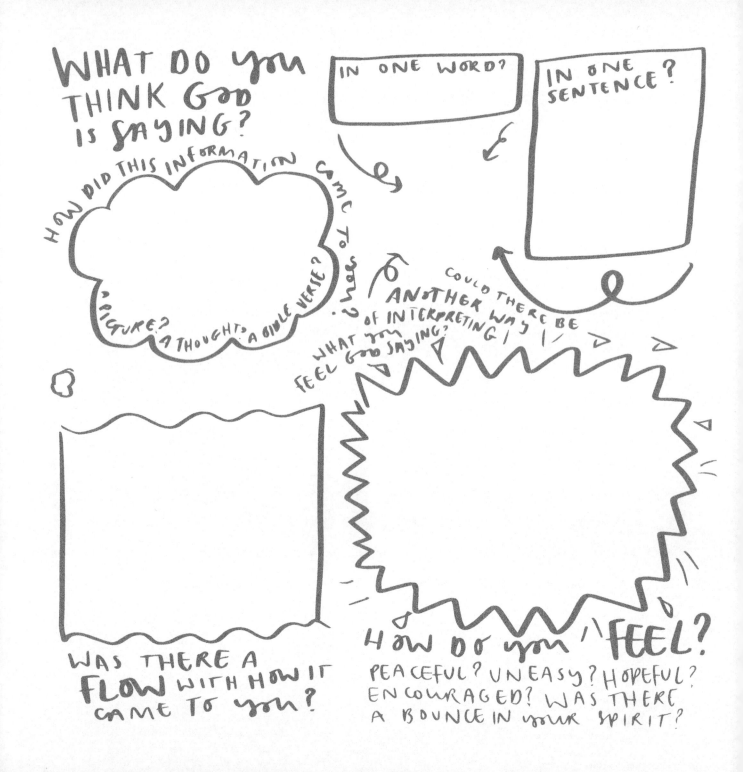

DOES IT FIT WITH WHAT THE BIBLE TEACHES? WHAT DO GODLY FRIENDS THINK?

DO YOU NEED TO ASK GOD ANY MORE QUESTIONS? TO HELP YOU UNDERSTAND/GET MORE DETAIL...?

DO YOU NEED TO ACT ON ANYTHING HE HAS SAID?

FOLLOW UP.
DID YOU GET ANYTHING RIGHT/WRONG? WHAT CAN I LEARN?

CONFIDENCE SCALE

10 Extremely sure

0 Very unsure

DATE: / /

Date _____ / _____ / _____

RIPE BANANAS

"As iron sharpens iron, so one person sharpens another."
Proverbs 27:17

Bananas contain a hormone (ethylene) that not only causes its own ripening but also the ripening of the fruit around it. In a similar way, God often works through His people to bring about a maturing, equipping and 'ripening' of others.

REFLECT
What is one area that you really want to grow in?

ACT
If you don't already have this in your life, think about someone who would be willing to meet with you in order to help you grow and 'ripen' in your faith.

Date _____ / _____ / _____

AWAKENED EARS

"The Sovereign Lord has given me a well-instructed tongue, to know the word that sustains the weary. He wakens me morning by morning, wakens my ear to listen like one being instructed."
Isaiah 50:4

Life can be exhausting and hard. This can make us feel weary and lost sometimes. Hebrews 3:13 says that we should, *"encourage one another daily".*

REFLECT
Imagine what your life could look like if you began each day by asking and listening to God for His instructions.

ACT
Ask God to put into your mind someone who really needs some words of encouragement right now. Then ask God what He wants to say. Write them a card and include what you felt in it.

THEIR NAME: _____

GOD SAYS

Date _____ / _____ / _____

WORDS OF FIRE

"Is not my word like fire," declares the LORD, "and like a hammer that breaks a rock in pieces?"
Jeremiah 23:29

God's words are powerful. God's words spoken through you are also very powerful. It isn't about how many words we speak, it's about them coming right from the heart of God. One word from God is more powerful than a thousand nice, well-meaning words that aren't from God.

REFLECT
God's word is like fire. It can provide warmth, security and light, but it can also burn away the unwanted rubbish.

ACT
Ask God to put someone on your heart. Ask Him for just one word for that person. Share it with them.

Record their feedback here.

WHAT YOU SAID TO _____

THEIR FEEDBACK

Date ____ / ____ / ____

TRUSTWORTHY TROOPERS

"I will put my words in his mouth. He will tell them everything I command him."
Deuteronomy 18:18

God wants to use us to speak His words to the world around us. However in order to do this we need to be faithful and trustworthy stewards with those words, resisting the urge to exaggerate or embellish what He has given us. Luke 16:10 says *"Whoever can be trusted with very little can also be trusted with much, and whoever is dishonest with very little will also be dishonest with much."*

REFLECT
Look back over your life. Have there been times when you've exaggerated a story or experience to make yourself look or sound better, or for it to somehow seem more dramatic or impressive?

ACT
Are there certain situations or people who make it more likely that you will not tell the entire truth somehow?

Write them down here.

I AM TEMPTED TO NOT SPEAK THE TRUTH WHEN...

- ✗ _____
- ✗ _____
- ✗ _____
- ✗ _____
- ✗ _____

Date _____ / _____ / _____

FAITHFUL STEWARDS

"His master replied, 'Well done, good and faithful servant! You have been faithful with a few things; I will put you in charge of many things. Come and share your master's happiness!"
Matthew 25:23

Imagine if Pablo Picasso gave you his house and all his art supplies for a year and asked you create something beautiful, but all you did was to sharpen a pencil. Or imagine if the British Museum gave you 24 hour lifetime access to every exhibition, but you never left the front doormat. What a waste, what a waste! Everything we have is on loan to us from God since everything belongs to Him. But God expects us to use what we've been given.

REFLECT

Do you think that you are making the most out of everything that you have been given - money, opportunities, education, relationships etc.?

ACT

Write a list of everything you feel like God has given you to steward - big and small.

Ask the Holy Spirit to help you to be faithful with all these things.

FAITHFULNESS

Date ____ / ____ / ____

WHOSE APPROVAL?

"Am I now trying to win the approval of human beings, or of God? Or am I trying to please people? If I were still trying to please people, I would not be a servant of Christ."
Galatians 1:10

Whatever your age, peer pressure is all around us. People will want you to do things and say things that God is not asking you to do or say. We need to resist this urge and temptation.

The fear of God, not people, should motivate us in all things. Our primary desire should be for God's approval rather than man's.

REFLECT
Meditate on this verse: "It is dangerous to be concerned with what others think of you, but if you trust the LORD, you are safe." (Proverbs 29:25, GNT)

ACT
Ask God to search your heart. Whose approval matters to you most?

Date _____ / _____ / _____

PERMISSION

"These are the things you are to do: Speak the truth to each other."
Zechariah 8:16

I wore braces for three years in order to straighten my wonky teeth. When they were taken off my orthodontist told me to wear a retainer at night in order to stop my teeth from moving back. But I didn't wear them as often as I should have. As a result, some of my teeth became crooked again. The Bible says that we need one another in order to keep walking in God's straight path of righteousness. If we walk alone, we risk taking a crooked route.

REFLECT
We need to give permission to others to speak truth to us and we need to be honest and open about our lives.

ACT
Name someone who you can be really honest with and who could help you live a godly life.

NAME: _____

CAN SPEAK HONESTLY INTO MY LIFE

Date _____ / _____ / _____

KEEPING ON TRACK

"The ear that listens to life-giving reproof will dwell among the wise. Whoever ignores instruction despises himself, but he who listens to reproof gains intelligence."
Proverbs 15:31-32 (ESV)

In air navigation, experts have a rule of thumb known as the '1 in 60 rule'. This rule states that for every 1 degree a plane veers off its course, it misses its target destination by 1 mile for every 60 miles you fly. Ultimately, this means that the further you travel, the further you are from your desired destination. Knowing when we've gone off track, and making adjustments to keep us in the right direction, is important if we want to learn how God is speaking to us.

REFLECT
Are you afraid of receiving feedback? Do you actively seek it?

ACT
Whenever you share something you feel God is saying to you, try to obtain specific, detailed feedback about what you said.

Record it and try to learn from it.

Date _____ / _____ / _____

GIVING FEEDBACK

"Therefore encourage one another and build each other up, just as in fact you are doing."
1 Thessalonians 5:11

We've talked about the importance of receiving feedback on the things that we've done and said so that we can learn and grow. It's also really kind and helpful for others when we do the same for them.

REFLECT
Has anyone ever shared anything with you that they felt was from God? If so, did you thank them and give them any helpful reflections and insight on what/how they shared?

ACT
Take some time to give someone some detailed encouragement.

WHO?

> FEEDBACK...

Date _____ / _____ / _____

PASSING IT ON

"Therefore go and make disciples of all nations"
Matthew 28:19

As Christians, we're all called to make disciples. A true disciple is not just a student or a learner, but a follower: one who applies what they have learnt. Helping to disciple someone doesn't need to be difficult and we're not expected to be experts. Sometimes discipleship can simply look like passing on the one thing that we learnt yesterday in order to help someone else live in that truth today.

REFLECT
Look back on your journey through this book and identify the key things that you have learnt so far.

ACT
What one bit of advice do you think you could pass on to someone else that might help them on their own journey of listening and connecting to God?

Date ____ / ____ / ____

RELATIONAL REDWOODS

"And let us consider how we may spur one another on toward love and good deeds, not giving up meeting together, as some are in the habit of doing, but encouraging one another".
Hebrews 10:24-25

The tallest tree in the world is named Hyperion. It's a Giant Redwood and reaches 379.7 feet. Redwoods are incredible survivors and can live to be 2,000 years old! Interestingly, given how tall they are, they do not have a vertical root like other trees. Their roots are actually very shallow. What holds them up are their horizontal roots which intertwine with the roots of other redwoods. These connections then form a mat and this matting anchors all the trees together.

REFLECT
What are your 'lateral roots' like? Are you connected to church family or are you isolated? A tree with poor roots is vulnerable.

ACT
Being part of a church family will help us as we listen to God's voice. What one step can you take today that will strengthen your roots?

WHAT ARE YOUR ROOTS LIKE?

Date _____ / _____ / _____

GUT HEALTH

"Above all else, guard your heart, for everything you do flows from it."
Proverbs 4:23

Did you know that the gut is directly connected to the brain? In fact, the gut has as many neurones as a cat's brain![1] If you eat food that isn't healthy, your good gut bacteria can become sick. If your gut is sick, it will affect your brain, which in turn affects your entire body.

REFLECT
What are you 'feeding' on? It might be that you are watching, reading and thinking about things that are making your heart and mind sick. Should you consider changing your 'diet'?

ACT
Pray - Father, I give you my spiritual stomach and what I fill myself with. Help me to honour and worship you with my choices. Amen.

---

1 Read Michael Moseley's book Clever Guts diet for more fascinating facts about the gut.

Date ____ / _____ / _____

ADDICTION

"It is for freedom that Christ has set us free. Stand firm, then, and do not let yourselves be burdened again by a yoke of slavery."
Galatians 5:1

Did you know that research suggests that sugar is as addictive as certain drugs like cocaine?[1] Jesus came to set us free from the power of sin and death. God doesn't want us to be addicted to anything except for being with Him and talking to Him.

REFLECT
Are there things in your life that are producing an addiction in you?

ACT
Spend some time writing down the things that you may have an unhealthy attachment to e.g. computer gaming or social media. Ask God what He wants you to do about those things.

1   Dinicolantonio, J., O'Keefe, J. and Wilson, W. (2017) Sugar addiction: Is it real? A narrative review. British Journal of Sports Medicine, 52 (14).

WHAT ARE your SUGAR CUBES?

Date ____ / ____ / ____

DISAPPOINTMENT

"'For my thoughts are not your thoughts, neither are your ways my ways,' declares the Lord."
Isaiah 55:8-9

Part of walking in our Christian faith is knowing that there will always be mystery involved. We cannot expect to understand everything that God does and says because He is God and we are not. He knows, sees and understands things that we do not. God simply doesn't have the same perspective as we do. Sometimes this will be difficult for us because we will be left with unanswered questions.

REFLECT
Have you ever really wanted God to speak to you about something but He has stayed silent about it and spoken to you about something else entirely?

ACT
Set aside your own agenda today. Spend some time asking God what He wants to talk to you about right now. Were you surprised by what He wanted you to focus on?

GOD SAID...

Date _____ / _____ / _____

SOFT HEARTS

"Today, if you hear his voice, do not harden your hearts"
Psalm 95:8

Sometimes we might feel as though God is asking, or has asked, us to do something, but we don't want to do it for some reason. For example, perhaps God is encouraging you to forgive someone who He keeps putting into your mind, but that person brought you great pain in the past.

REFLECT
Meditate on 2 John 1:6, "And this is love: that we walk in obedience to his commands."

ACT
Ask the Holy Spirit to show you any area of your life where you may have hardened your heart towards what He has been trying to say to you. Ask Him what you need to do about it.

WHERE IS YOUR HEART HARD?

Date _____ / _____ / _____

SPIRIT-FILLED SAILS

"And you will receive the gift of the Holy Spirit. The promise is for you and your children and for all who are far off—for all whom the Lord our God will call."
Acts 2:38-39

Acts 2:2 says, *"Suddenly a sound like the blowing of a violent wind came from heaven and filled the whole house where they were sitting."* Just as a sail needs to be constantly filled with wind in order to keep the boat moving, we too need to be constantly filled with the Holy Spirit.

REFLECT
What do your 'Spirit-sails' look like? Are they flat and flapping or are they stretched and full?

ACT
Have you been filled with the Holy Spirit? If you haven't, ask Him to fill you. If you have already been filled with the Spirit, ask Him to fill you in a fresh and powerful way.

Date _____ / _____ / _____

WEATHER WARNINGS

"For our struggle is not against flesh and blood, but against the rulers, against the authorities, against the powers of this dark world and against the spiritual forces of evil in the heavenly realms."
Ephesians 6:12

If you've ever watched the weather forecast, you may have seen that when a cold front of air meets a hot front, there's often turbulent weather. As Christians, we have the Holy Spirit living in us. This is a bit like the warm front. Sometimes, because of the way we are (or have been) living, the enemy can have a certain influence on us. When this happens there is a conflict. It feels like a battle is going on. This is because the Holy Spirit wants to be the only influence in your life!

REFLECT

Do you feel as though any part of your life feels a bit stormy? This might be because the Holy Spirit is at work.

ACT

Ask the Holy Spirit to show you any part of your life that is not completely under His influence. Invite the Holy Spirit to have total control of that area of your body, heart or mind.

WARM

COLD

✓ Write opposing things here

Date _____ / _____ / _____

GIFT OF LANGUAGES

"Now to each one the manifestation of the Spirit is given for the common good. To one there is given through the Spirit a message of wisdom... to another speaking in different kinds of tongues".
1 Corinthians 12: 7-10

Sometimes when I really want to hear from God but feel a bit stuck, I find that praying in my heavenly language (or the "gift of tongues") really helps me.

REFLECT
Meditate on Acts 2:4:

"All of them were filled with the Holy Spirit and began to speak in other tongues as the Spirit enabled them."

ACT
If you don't have the gift but would like it, why don't you ask the Holy Spirit if He would give it to you? It really helps you to connect to God's heart and mind[1].

---

1 Practical Tip - God doesn't take over your body and start moving your mouth like a puppet! Begin by opening your mouth and speaking out whatever words that come. This is an act of faith, so try not to think about it too much. Once you have a few words, keep going. Don't give up. It's a gift to grow in, so keep practicing just as you would any other ability.

USE THIS PAGE TO DRAW/WRITE THE DIFFERENT WAYS YOU ENJOY WORSHIPPING GOD

Date ____ / ____ / ____

SEND ME!

"Then I heard the voice of the Lord saying, "Whom shall I send? And who will go for us?" And I said, "Here am I. Send me!"
Isaiah 6:8

God is looking for (imperfect) people who will make themselves available for Him to use. If we're willing for God to use us, we must leave space for Him to do the unexpected.

REFLECT
When it comes to God's involvement in your life, do you expect the unexpected?

ACT
This week, make an intentional effort to leave extra room in your day, if possible. Turn up early to events, if you have any.

What are your observations?

Date _____ / _____ / _____

YES OR NO?

"But seek first his kingdom and his righteousness, and all these things will be given to you as well."
Matthew 6:33

Busyness can rob us of God appointed interactions and opportunities. When our life is full of our plans, sometimes that leaves no room for God's agenda. For every 'yes' we make, we are saying a thousand 'no's to other things.

REFLECT
What things are you saying 'yes' to at the moment? What things are you saying 'no' to? Does anything need to change in your life?

ACT
Ask God what He wants you to prioritise right now. Record your 'yes' and 'no' responses.

YES!	NO!

Date _____ / _____ / _____

SMELLY LIVES

"For we are to God the pleasing aroma of Christ among those who are being saved and those who are perishing."
2 Corinthians 2:15

When my son is in deep sleep and and nothing will awaken him, I start to cook bacon. The smell of it wakes him up every time! The passage we just read tells us that as you go about your everyday, normal life, you carry the fragrance of Jesus with you. Sometimes the Holy Spirit will allow others to smell that fragrance, awakening in them a desire and hunger to know what that smell is all about. This can be an opportunity for you to share your faith with them.

REFLECT
Have you noticed anyone recently who doesn't know Jesus but seems to want to be spending more time with you?

ACT
Write down their name here. Perhaps this is the Holy Spirit moving through you to stir in them a desire to know more about Jesus. Spend some time praying for them.

WHO IS SMELLING YOUR LIFE?

Date _____ / _____ / _____

TURN RIGHT, THEN LEFT

"Whether you turn to the right or to the left, your ears will hear a voice behind you, saying, "This is the way; walk in it.""
Isaiah 30:21

Recently, I went for a walk but right at the beginning of it I really intentionally asked the Holy Spirit to guide my footsteps in the way He wanted me to go. I had no agenda other than to try to learn how to listen for His directions with each step. On that walk, I bumped into four different, separate people all of whom I ended up having very significant conversations with.

REFLECT
The Holy Spirit loves it when we intentionally invite Him to guide us in the big and little steps of our life.

ACT
Go for a walk today and ask the Holy Spirit to direct you. As you walk, ask Him why He is taking you on this route.

WHAT MOMENTS HAS GOD GIVEN YOU?

Date _____ / _____ / _____

GOD'S GROCERY SHOP

"Because he turned his ear to me, I will call on him as long as I live."
Psalm 116:2

God doesn't want to micromanage every area of our lives like a controlling dictator. But He does want an ever-growing, ever-deepening relationship with us. This means that God is interested in sharing in the small things of our lives, just as a true friend would be. Does God care about your weekly food shop? Yes, because He might want to add to it to show His love to someone. A well-timed chocolate bar to the right person might be exactly what they need to cheer them up.

REFLECT
God loves to be welcomed into all aspects of your life, even the boring parts like grocery shopping! Listening to Him at all times can turn the mundane into meaningful.

ACT
The next time you go shopping spend a few moments beforehand asking God if He wants to add anything to your list.

Date ____ / _____ / _____

GOD OF THE WEAK

""My grace is sufficient for you, for my power is made perfect in weakness." Therefore I will boast all the more gladly about my weaknesses, so that Christ's power may rest on me."
2 Corinthians 12:9

I have a great fear of public speaking. That's why I like writing; because then I can communicate without people looking at me. However, I also feel God has been giving me opportunities to speak publicly in person. For me, this is very scary. In those moments I really have to ask God to be strong on my behalf because all I want to do is hide in the loo.

REFLECT
Do you have any thing/s about you or your life that makes you feel disqualified from God using you?

ACT
Write down those weaknesses. Then pray that God's power would be made perfect in those things.

Abraham was old
Sara was impatient
Jacob was a cheater
Gideon was insecure
Peter had a temper
Noah got drunk
Jonah ran from God
Paul was a murderer
Miriam was a gossip
Zaccheus was short
David had an affair
Martha was a worrier
Thomas was a doubter
Moses stuttered
Elijah was moody
Lazarus was dead

MY WEAKNESS IS:

Date _____ / _____ / _____

SEARCH ME

"Search me, God, and know my heart; test me and know my anxious thoughts. See if there is any offensive way in me and lead me in the way everlasting."
Psalm 139:23-24

Magnetic resonance imaging (MRI) is a type of scan. It uses strong magnetic fields and radio waves to produce detailed images of the inside of the body. It can be used to help diagnose problems that we can't see with our eyes. The Holy Spirit is even more powerful. He knows the depths of our hearts and minds. He sees when we are thinking or feeling things that are coming from a place of brokenness and sin. Since sin always causes destruction, the Spirit wants to help show us these things.

REFLECT
Spend some time by yourself today and invite the Holy Spirit to search your heart and mind.

ACT
Ask Him to show you if there are any areas of your life that need to change. Are you willing to turn away from these things? Ask Jesus for His forgiveness, if necessary.

WRITE WHAT THINGS NEED TO CHANGE

Date _____ / _____ / _____

CHARACTER REFLECTIONS

"And we all, who with unveiled faces contemplate the Lord's glory, are being transformed into his image with ever-increasing glory"
2 Corinthians 3:18

Have you ever been really irritated by someone and not known why? We are being transformed into being more like Jesus everyday. Sometimes God uses other people to be like a mirror showing us what we can be like. Once we have an awareness of this, we can ask Jesus to help us be more like Him in that area.

REFLECT
Can you think of anyone you know who makes you think, "I can be a bit like that sometimes."

ACT
Spend some time with God and ask Him whether He is trying to highlight an aspect of your character that needs to change. Ask Him to help you be more Christ-like in this area.

IN THE MIRROR OF OTHERS, I SEE...

Date ____ / _____ / _____

OPEN DOORS

"I went to Troas to preach the gospel of Christ and found that the Lord had opened a door for me"
2 Corinthians 2:12

The Holy Spirit sometimes guides us by providing us with doors of opportunity. When God wants to lead us into something new, we don't have to strive or force our way through those doors because He opens them for us. If we are unsure, He is able to guide us by His peace.

REFLECT
Meditate on 2 Corinthians 3:18, "a great door for effective work has opened to me."

Have any new opportunities become available to you recently?

ACT
Ask God what doors He has placed before you. Ask Him whether they are doors to walk through now, or in the future.

DOORS TO OPEN

Date _____ / _____ / _____

CLOSED DOORS

"And they went through the region of Phrygia and Galatia, having been forbidden by the Holy Spirit to speak the word in Asia."
Acts 16:6 (ESV)

There's a difference between an entrance and exit door. Exit doors are designed to let you out and to keep you from coming back in. Sometimes the Holy Spirit opens doors for us. But sometimes He guides us by closing doors that we might want to, or try to, walk through.

REFLECT
Are you trying to pursue something that you feel should be opening up for you, but instead feels like you're walking into a brick wall?

ACT
Spend some time in prayer and ask the Holy Spirit to bring into your mind any areas of your life that He is closing to you.

DOORS TO CLOSE

Date ____ / ____ / ____

WHAT'S IN A NAME?

"No longer will you be called Abram; your name will be Abraham, for I have made you a father of many nations."
Genesis 17:5

Before you were born God knew what you were going to be called. In the Bible, names were considered to be very important because they often had a prophetic element to them.

REFLECT
Can you think of any Bible stories where the name of the person was significant in some way?

ACT
Look up the meaning of your name. Ask God about it from His perspective.

HELLO MY NAME IS.

my NAME MEANS...

GOD IS SAYING...

Date _____ / _____ / _____

A TIME FOR...

"There is a time for everything, and a season for every activity under the heavens."
Ecclesiastes 3:1

Whether we like it or not, life is full of change. In hot weather, we can wear t-shirts to help keep us cool, in cold weather we can wear thick coats. Wisdom is knowing what is appropriate for today. God can give us that wisdom.

REFLECT
Do you adjust to change easily or are you resistant to it?

ACT
Read Ecclesiastes 3.

Ask the Holy Spirit for His wisdom and to show you which verse is important for you right now.

"There is a time for everything,
   and a season for every activity under the heavens:
   A time to be born and a time to die,
   A time to plant and a time to uproot,
   A time to kill and a time to heal,
   A time to tear down and a time to build,
   A time to weep and a time to laugh,
   A time to mourn and a time to dance,
   A time to scatter stones and a time to gather them,
   A time to embrace and a time to refrain from embracing,
   A time to search and a time to give up,
   A time to keep and a time to throw away,
   A time to tear and a time to mend,
   A time to be silent and a time to speak,
   A time to love and a time to hate,
   A time for war and a time for peace."

Date ____ / ____ / ____

ODD EXPERIENCES

"Moses thought, "I will go over and see this strange sight—why the bush does not burn up." When the Lord saw that he had gone over to look, God called to him from within the bush, "Moses! Moses!" And Moses said, "Here I am.""
Exodus 3:3-4

God sometimes tries to get our attention through experiences that He knows will seem a bit out-of-the-blue, unusual or strange to us somehow. He's hoping that it will cause us to turn to Him and ask Him what He wants to say.

REFLECT
Think about the last few weeks. Has anything odd happened to you or around you? Was there something that made you think, 'that's weird!' or that just stood out somehow?

ACT
Write down anything that made an impression on you and then ask God what He is trying to say.

ODD THINGS ?/?
KEEP A LIST

Date _____ / _____ / _____

REPETITION REPETITION

"The word of the LORD came to me: "What do you see, Jeremiah?""
Jeremiah 1:11

Another way God might try to get your attention is through repetition. Perhaps it's something you keep seeing, a person you keep bumping into or a phrase you keep hearing.

REFLECT
Have you been aware of any repetitions lately? Some things will be due to natural random chance, but it might also be God.

ACT
Over the next week, pay attention to patterns and repetitions that happen around you. Jot them down. Ask God if He's trying to say something.

REPEAT
REPEAT
REPEAT
REPEAT
REPEAT
REPEAT

KEEP NOTE

Date _____ / _____ / _____

FULL OF FRUITS

"But the fruit of the Spirit is love, joy, peace, patience, kindness, goodness, faithfulness, gentleness, self-control; against such things there is no law."
Galatians 5:22-23

As Christians we have the Holy Spirit in us. The evidence, or fruits, of the Spirit at work in us should be visible to others. Jesus was full of the Spirit (Luke 4:1). Jesus would therefore have been the most loving, joyful, peaceful, patient, kind, good, faithful, gentle, self-controlled person you would have ever met.

REFLECT
Do you think that people who know you well would be able to say that you are e.g. more joyful than their other non-believing friends?

ACT
Ask God which fruit of the Spirit He is trying to ripen in you at the moment. God wants us to be 'trees' that bear all His fruits and not just one. They are all important to Him.

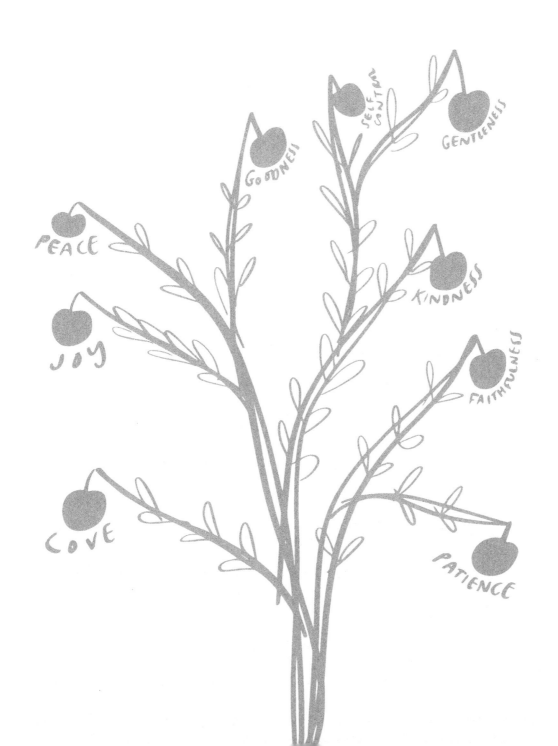

Date _____ / _____ / _____

SEASONS

"When a farmer ploughs for planting, does he plough continually? Does he keep on breaking up and working the soil? … His God instructs him and teaches him the right way."
Isaiah 28:23-26

In life there are natural seasons that annually take place: spring, summer, autumn and winter. There are seasons for ploughing, sowing, weeding and harvesting. There are seasons of drought, monsoon, hurricanes and clear blue skies.

Life can be like that. Every season has its purpose and what we do in them changes.

REFLECT
What season do you think you're in right now?

ACT
Ask God what's the main thing He's trying to teach you or grow in you right now.

PLOUGHING?

SOWING?

WHICH SEASON ARE YOU IN?

HARVESTING?

WEEDING?

Date _____ / _____ / _____

GEAR CHANGE

"The power of the LORD came on Elijah and, tucking his cloak into his belt, he ran ahead of Ahab all the way to Jezreel."
1 Kings 18:46

In a manual car there are six gears. They determine how fast you go and what direction you go in. Sometimes God takes us through different gear changes. At points He might want us to go slowly, sometimes we might need to reflect and look back. Other times He might want us to go as fast as we can. It's important that we listen carefully to God about what pace He wants us to go at and when we should change gears.

REFLECT
What gear do you think you're in right now?

ACT
Ask God whether He wants you to change gear.

REALLY FAST!

5

4

3

2

START

| 1 | 3 | 5 |
| 2 | 4 | R |

LOOK BACK

Date _____ / _____ / _____

PERSEVERE

""Go and look toward the sea," he told his servant. And he went up and looked. "There is nothing there," he said. Seven times Elijah said, "Go back.""
1 Kings 18:43

In 1 Kings 18 we read about when Elijah prayed for rain. It goes like this:

Elijah prayed, no cloud. Prayed, no cloud. Prayed, no cloud. Prayed, no cloud. Prayed, no cloud. Prayed, no cloud. Prayed, tiny cloud.

Then it poured.

REFLECT
What are the things that you are praying about at the moment that don't seem to be resulting in any change? Are there things that you have given up on?

ACT
Write down these things. Don't give up! Every prayer is heard.

Sometimes God is waiting for the right time and then it will pour.

Date _____ / _____ / _____

TRAFFIC LIGHTS

"Wait for the Lord and keep His way"
Psalm 37:34 (ESV)

Timing is important, isn't it? If you drive during a red light you could crash. Just like when you drive along a road and you have to pay attention to the traffic lights, so too with life. Sometimes God wants you to faithfully continue doing what you're already doing. Sometimes He wants you to prepare, or get ready for change. Other times God wants you to put certain things on hold, either momentarily or permanently.

REFLECT
What do you find harder: to start something new, stop something old or keep doing the same thing?

ACT
Make a list of all the things you have going on in your life. For each of them ask God whether it's a red, green or amber light; stop, go or wait.

Date ____ / ____ / ____

GOD'S HOME

"Here I am! I stand at the door and knock. If anyone hears my voice and opens the door, I will come in and eat with that person, and they with me."
Revelation 3:20

When my children have friends over we like to welcome them warmly into our home. We want them to feel really comfortable in it. However, we ask everyone not to play in our main bedroom because that's *'our space'.*

When we become Christians, we invite Jesus to be King (or have ownership) of our lives and to come and live inside us by His Spirit. This makes us *'temples of the Holy Spirit'* (1 Corinthians 6:19).

REFLECT
Even though we invite Jesus to live in our 'house', this doesn't necessarily mean that we give Him access to every 'room', or area, of our life.

ACT
Ask the Holy Spirit to show you whether you have allowed him to go into all of the rooms in your life.

Is there any area to which you are not giving Him the keys?

WHICH ROOMS ARE OPEN?
WHICH ARE LOCKED?

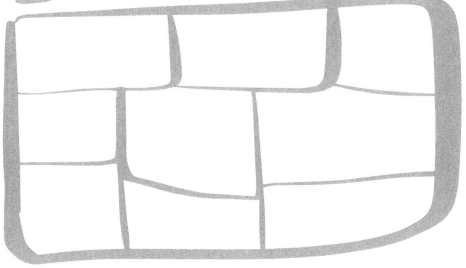

Date ____ / ____ / ____

FAREWELL, CATERPILLAR

"Therefore, if anyone is in Christ, he is a new creation. The old has passed away; behold, the new has come"
2 Corinthians 5:17

Although it can be a bit hard to understand, the Bible tells us that when we become a Christian, even though we look the same on the outside, we actually become a 'new creation' spiritually.

I find using the analogy of a caterpillar (old self) and a butterfly (new-self) helpful. The cocoon to me represents the significance behind water baptism (identifying with Christ's death and dying with Him).

REFLECT
Even though we become butterflies at our conversion, we can sometimes be so used to being and thinking like a caterpillar that we need to change the way we think.

ACT
Record any 'old caterpillar' thoughts you think you might still be having that aren't part of the new creation that God has made you to be.

Date _____ / _____ / _____

HELLO, BUTTERFLY

"You were taught, with regard to your former way of life, to put off your old self, which is being corrupted by its deceitful desires; to be made new in the attitude of your minds; and to put on the new self"
Ephesians 4:22-24

The Christian life is one of cooperating with the Spirit in order that the new self we have now become in Christ develops and grows to maturity while the 'old self' is stripped away. Our will is freed from being bound to sin, but we can still choose to walk God's way or to give in to our flesh or the devil. The greatest battlefield with this all is often in the mind. The passage we read today is about renewing our mind and learning to think God's way and do things God's way.

REFLECT
Meditate on Romans 12:2, "Do not conform to the pattern of this world, but be transformed by the renewing of your mind."

ACT
What patterns of this world are surrounding you? Are you following them, or are you following God's pattern? Record them and then spend some time praying into them.

Date _____ / _____ / _____

MIND OF CHRIST

"We demolish arguments and every pretension that sets itself up against the knowledge of God, and we take captive every thought to make it obedient to Christ."
2 Corinthians 10:5

Quality control is the process used by a manufacturer or organisation to make sure that the quality of a product or service is up to their standards.

The verse we've read tells us that we need to capture every single one of our catapulting thoughts. Then, with the Spirit's help, we need to test and inspect them against God's lens of truth, The Bible.

REFLECT
Do you think your thoughts meet God's quality control standards?

ACT
Ask God to bring into your mind any thoughts that need to be locked up because they're not aligned with Christ's way of thinking.

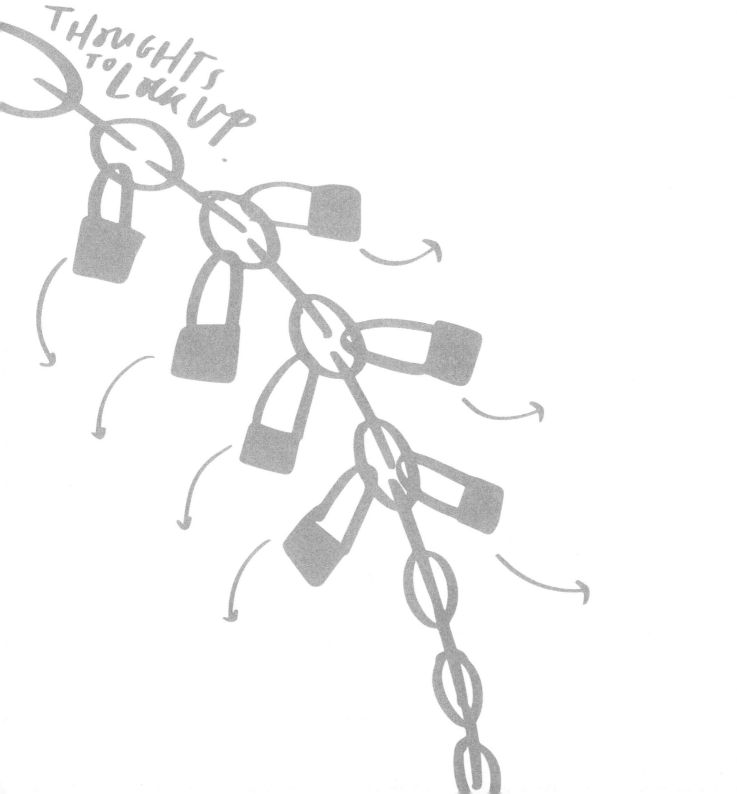

Date _____ / _____ / _____

STAY IN YOUR LANE

"For we are God's handiwork, created in Christ Jesus to do good works, which God prepared in advance for us to do."
Ephesians 2:10

Have you ever seen a sprinter running on a track in the Olympics? They each have their own lane to run in with clear boundaries. They need to stay in their lane because if they don't they could trip up the other contestants. Each of us have been given *'good works'* that God has prepared for us to do. Only you can do what God has planned for you and it's important that we don't get sidetracked or distracted by things that aren't meant for us.

REFLECT
Do you compare yourself to others and try to be like them at the expense of using and doing what God has put before you?

ACT
What things do you think God has put in your 'lane'? Write these things down and ask God for His help to do these things faithfully.

WHAT's IN your LANE?

Date _____ / _____ / _____

KINTSUKUROI

"Yet you, Lord, are our Father. We are the clay, you are the potter; we are all the work of your hand."
Isaiah 64:8

Kintsukuroi means 'to repair with gold'. It's the art of repairing pottery with gold or silver lacquer with the understanding that the piece is more beautiful for having been broken. Even when we feel like broken bits of pottery, Jesus can work in us and through us in a way that lets His light shine through in a beautiful way. He wants us to offer our broken bits to Him so that He can bring healing and restoration.

REFLECT
Ask Jesus to show you any areas of your life that need His healing hands.

ACT
Invite the Holy Spirit to bring healing to your broken areas.

No-one is ever too broken for God to heal. There is always hope.

Date ____ / ____ / ____

FOLLOW THE CLOUD

"Whenever the cloud lifted from above the tent, the Israelites set out; wherever the cloud settled, the Israelites encamped."
Numbers 9:17

In Numbers 9 you can read some of the story of how God led the Israelites in the wilderness. When God's presence (represented by a pillar of cloud) moved, the Israelites were to move. When it settled, they were to stay. Sometimes it rested in one place just overnight, but other times it remained for days or months. No-one could predict how long they were going to be in one place, they just had to keep their focus on the cloud and move as it moved.

REFLECT
Learning to recognise when God's blessing has shifted is important so we don't end up with empty 'tents'. Has God moved on from something that you're still holding on to?

ACT
Ask Jesus to help you move forward and follow His lead and direction. Ask the Spirit to help you know when it's time to leave the things of yesterday behind.

IS THERE ANY AREA WHERE GOD HAS MOVED FROM BUT YOU HAVEN'T?

write here

Date _____ / _____ / _____

MY HANDS

"Therefore, I urge you, brothers and sisters, in view of God's mercy, to offer your bodies as a living sacrifice, holy and pleasing to God—this is your true and proper worship."
Romans 12:1

Our whole body is made up of many parts. Each part has a unique role to play. In the next few pages, we will focus on the different parts of the body and ask God to use them for His glory. We're going to begin by focusing on our hands.

REFLECT
Jesus often reached out His compassionate hands to bring healing, love and reconciliation to others. He wants to use your hands to do the same.

ACT
This week, ask God to specifically use your hands to bless someone in need.

Date ____ / ____ / ____

MY FEET

"Since we live by the Spirit, let us keep in step with the Spirit."
Galatians 5:25

Imagine if you were blind. You would be completely dependent on someone else, or something else (e.g. a guide dog), to help you.

In many ways, we are actually a bit blind - we have a very limited view of our past, present and future. Part of walking with God is about allowing Him to take the lead and guide us in our every day steps because He sees and knows everything. As we surrender our ways to Him, He directs us.

REFLECT

Pray - Holy Spirit, show me how to walk with you; not ahead, or behind, but completely in step with you. I give you my feet - take me wherever you want. Lead me and guide me. Amen.

ACT

Wherever you walk, you represent Jesus to the world around you.

Write down one specific way you can represent Jesus today.

Date _____ / _____ / _____

MY HEART

"'Love the Lord your God with all your heart and with all your soul and with all your mind and with all your strength.' The second is this: 'Love your neighbour as yourself.'"
Mark 12:30-31

God wants to have the highest place of affection in your heart. But He also wants you to love yourself, because He created you. And He wants you to love others, because He created them. Love matters to God, but He needs to come first.

REFLECT
What do you struggle to love about yourself? Who do you struggle to love? Do you find it hard to tell God that you love Him?

ACT
Spend some time expressing your love for God in whatever way feels most natural to you. You may choose to sing, write, meditate or draw. It doesn't matter how you do it, as long as you are sincere.

I GIVE you my HEART

↳ for myself

↳ for others

and above all you ↰

Date ____ / ____ / ____

MY SPINE

"Have I not commanded you? Be strong and courageous. Do not be afraid; do not be discouraged, for the LORD your God will be with you wherever you go."
Joshua 1:9

What things scare you? It might be having conversations with strangers or public speaking. Sometimes God wants us to do things that might make us tremble! Being scared doesn't mean we shouldn't do them though.

REFLECT
Pray - Holy Spirit, please strengthen me with boldness to take risks so that Jesus can be glorified. I want to live a life that enables you to do the impossible things that only you can do. Amen.

ACT
Do you shy away from taking risks or embracing change? Have you got situations before you that you need to step into with courage? What one brave step can you take today?

I GIVE you my SPINE

Date ____ / ____ / ____

MY EYES

"But blessed are your eyes because they see, and your ears because they hear."
Matthew 13:16

When we ask the Holy Spirit to help us see things with the eyes of Jesus this can change everything. It can lead to moments of repentance in our day or experiencing heartbreak in the situations we see. It can mean noticing people and having time for them when we would normally rush by. It might mean taking a plank out of our own eye and being non judgemental. It could also mean speaking truth in love when we would normally stay quiet.

REFLECT
Do you think you are seeing and hearing God's way?

ACT
Pray - Father, I give you my eyes. Help me to look at people, situations and things the way you do. Where I am blind, help me to see. Amen.

Date ____ / ____ / ____

MY MOUTH

"Then the Lord reached out his hand and touched my mouth and said to me, "I have put my words in your mouth.""
Jeremiah 1:9

Whenever you see a police officer, you expect them to constantly be acting, speaking and responding in a way that demonstrates the training, code and values of the entire police force that they represent. I often think about myself in this way as a Christian. People are constantly watching us and as Christ's followers, we represent Jesus and His values all the time. This includes our words. What we say and what we don't say really matters.

REFLECT

Jesus, I give you my mouth. I want to speak your words. Teach me when to speak and when to stay silent. Help my voice be used for your glory and honour. Amen.

ACT

This week try to be really aware of the words you speak. Do they represent Jesus well? Are they bringing life? Does God want to add anything to what you're saying?

I GIVE you my MOUTH PLEASE BE IN MY WORDS

Date ____ / _____ / _____

MY BRAIN

"Do not conform to the pattern of this world, but be transformed by the renewing of your mind."
Romans 12:2

Did you know that the human brain contains approximately one hundred billion neurons? This is about the same as the number of stars in the Milky Way galaxy. God gave you your brain and He expects you to use it. It is an extremely powerful tool and it becomes even more powerful when we surrender it back to God.

REFLECT
Pray - Holy Spirit, I give you my brain. Sanctify my mind, my thinking and my imagination. Use it to create, problem solve, understand and think in a way that gives God glory. Amen.

ACT
Ask the Holy Spirit whether there's a particular skill that He wants you to learn that will somehow be useful for you in future. For example, you might feel He wants you to learn French.

I GIVE YOU my BRAIN

Date _____ / _____ / _____

MY ATTENTION & FOCUS

"Therefore, since we are surrounded by such a great cloud of witnesses, let us throw off everything that hinders and the sin that so easily entangles. And let us run with perseverance the race marked out for us, fixing our eyes on Jesus"
Hebrews 12:1-2

If I saw a bull charging at me, I'd run very fast in the opposite direction. But if I saw a sign saying, "Free chocolate!" I'd eagerly walk towards it.

What we look at determines our focus. What we focus on determines our direction. And how much we value what we focus on determines how fast we move. Jesus is our ultimate reward. He is worthy of all our attention. Our love for Him should make us run fast towards Him.

REFLECT
What things in your life are distracting you from your focus on Jesus? What things are affecting the way you run towards Him?

ACT
Imagine if you were told that Jesus was going to come back in your lifetime. How would that affect your lifestyle? What one thing would you do more? What one thing would you do less?

Date _____ / _____ / _____

MY ALL

"Love the Lord your God with all your heart and with all your soul and with all your mind and with all your strength."
Mark 12:30

Complete, total, entire, everything, 100%. There are many words that can be used to understand what 'all' means in this passage.

Jesus deserves the whole of our affection and life, not part of us, not most of us, but all of us.

REFLECT
Is there any part of you or any area of your life that you are keeping back from God?

ACT
Pray - God, I give you my all, every fibre of my being. Help me not to hold anything back from you. Help me to glorify you in everything I do, always. Amen

I GIVE you my ALL

89 THE LORDSHIP PRAYER

LORD Jesus Christ, I acknowledge my need of you and accept you as my SAVIOUR, my LORD and my DELIVERER, I invite you to be the LORD of the whole of my life:

LORD of my mind and my attitudes and my mental health
LORD of my body and my physical health
LORD of my spirit and all my worship
LORD of my family and all my relationships
LORD of my sexuality and all its expressions
LORD of my work and service for you
LORD of my material goods and needs
LORD of my finances
LORD of my emotions and all of my reactions
LORD of my will and all of my decisions
LORD of my manner and time of my death (Ps. 139:16)

Thank you that you shed your blood to set me free, Amen.[1]

---

1 Ellel Ministries, Lordship Prayer

WHICH LINE OF THE PRAYER STANDS OUT MOST?

ADD SOME REFLECTIONS

Lord of My Mind, Attitudes + Mental Health

Lord of My Body + Physical Health

Lord of my Spirit & All my Worship

LORD OF MY **FAMILY** + ALL MY **RELATIONSHIPS**

LORD OF MY SEXUALITY + ALL IT'S EXPRESSIONS

Lord of my Material Goods + Needs

Lord of my Finances

A FOND FAREWELL

Well done for taking the time to work through these pages and invest in your relationship with God! I hope that you've had fun listening and talking to Him. You've come to the end of this book, but the journey for you doesn't need to stop here. A life walking with God is an ongoing adventure, so keep going! Pass on all you've learnt to others and encourage them to grow in their own relationship as well.

Your Father in heaven wants to use you as part of His plan to bring His Kingdom here on earth. The more time you spend with Him learning to discern His heart, ways, voice and words, the easier it will be for you to recognise when the Holy Spirit is nudging you to do or say something on His behalf. You represent Jesus to the world around you and so the closer you get to Him, the better that representation will be as you become increasingly like Him.

You will never regret spending time God. Stay connected with Him and stay connected with those who love Him. This will ensure that your love for Him will always remain fresh and strong.

With love,

Anna

ABOUT US

ANNA GOODMAN

Anna was born in Honduras and is married to Daniel, who was born in Guinea Bissau, West Africa. Anna has also lived in Nepal, Belgium and Barbados. Her maternal grandmother was Swiss and she has Croatian and Swedish sisters-in-law. Both her parents are British. Anna now lives in Cambridge, which is both very international and very British at the same time - much like her heart!

Anna moved to the UK in 1996 to do her A-levels and then went to the University of St. Andrews, Scotland, to do a neuroscience degree. In 2002, she moved down to Cambridge to complete a PhD, which is when she met Daniel who now leads the church they attend.

The first time Anna can remember hearing from God was when she was eight years old. She's therefore a big believer that you're never too young to hear God's voice. She is currently focusing on raising her two young sons to grow up listening and responding to God's voice for themselves.

Blog and website: annagoodman.co.uk
Instagram: @annagoodman_writer

ASHLEY SIMPKINS

Ashley grew up in the wonderful city of Norwich. She spent most of her childhood drawing anywhere and everywhere, being creative (which was often very messy), reading many, many books and playing imaginative games.

Ashley studied graphic design at Coventry University and spent three years falling more in love with hand-lettering and illustration.

In 2019, Ashley moved to Cambridge for ID, (Intentional Discipleship, a Relational Mission year out) and spent a year intentionally pursuing God, serving the church and getting to know Anna... which is how Ashley ended up being asked to illustrate this very book. God has done more than she could have asked or imagined with her year!

Since illustrating Connected, Ashley has moved back to Coventry, got married, bought a house and has started a new job as a graphic designer and illustrator.

Website: ashleydrew.co.uk
Instagram: @ashleyjsimpkins

THANK YOU!

Jim and Hannah Overton, Kate Moore, Beth Sears, Jodi Peek and Miriam Ogborn - you are all amazing in your own different ways. Thank you for your various bits of advice, encouragement, wisdom and edits. You all have such a wealth of knowledge and experience. I am so grateful to be able to glean and grow from your Godly insights and alternative perspectives. Thank you.

Phil Wilthew - you may not have realised it but your prophetic word really helped to shape, refine and motivate me with writing Connected and this book. I'm very grateful that God uses people like you to speak to people like me in order to give them direction and strategy so that we can work alongside His Will. Thank you, Phil, for your faithfulness with serving the church.

Vera and Ugur Tuna - thank you for your friendship and encouragement with writing these books. Your supportive words have motivated me to keep going even when I've wanted to stop.

Daniel, you always challenge, champion and cheer me on. Thank you for choosing me.

Anna

Thank you to my wonderful parents for always encouraging my creativity (and for putting up with the trail of pencil sharpening, paint splodges, carpet stains, and 1000's of sheets of printing).

My wonderful church family at Jubilee Church Coventry, thank you for all the fun and joy you bring, the love you show me, and for helping me grow and fall more in love with Jesus.

Josh, thank you for loving me, encouraging me and for bringing much joy and laughter to my life. You are a more than I could have ever asked for or dreamed up.

Anna, thank you for inviting me join you on this adventure.

Ashley

Printed in Great Britain
by Amazon